Praise for

Linda's book has been uplifting to read and experience. I found the book inspiring, helping me understand that even with past pain issues, we can still become connected back into true ourselves.

Her words have a warmth that allowed me to settle into the message and connect on many levels. I have not had alcohol addictions but it resonated with another form of addiction that I have to work through. Thank you for exposing life for us to learn from.

—Diane Gysin, author of *HealingBodies Healing Souls*

From addiction to redemption, Linda Crose-Andersen reveals honest raw emotions as she carries us through her transformation.

Amazing Grace is a workbook for personal growth. Read this book to see and feel the importance of living in the NOW.

—Belinda Farrell, author of *Find Your Friggin' Joy*

Every rational person knows that drugs and alcohol, when abused, could destroy your life.

Unfortunately, when one is in the throes of drugs and/or alcohol addiction, rational thought, logic and even self-preservation take a back seat to the desire for poisonous destruction.

And often, also unfortunately, the message of survival and then recovery can't be heard until one is able to hear it.

The running hope is that those who need the message can come into the light before it's too late. And that's why the story of redemption and recovery needs to continue to be told in every way possible—there is someone out there who needs to hear it.

Linda's version needs to be read and needs to be heard. It may the vehicle by which the next person or group of persons hears what they need to hear to save their lives. Linda combines humor, honestly and compassion as she shares her important and intimate story of hope.

I strongly recommend that you read Linda's story.

—William K. Wesley, author of
Full Life Balance: The Five Keys to the Kingdom

Amazing Grace

A spiritual journey from addiction to enlightenment

Linda Crose-Andersen, MMsc, MHt

First Edition: March 17, 2015

ISBN-10:1508793972
ISBN-13:9781508793977

DEDICATION

"This book is dedicated to Alan Sherer, LCSW, who provided a lifetime of service as a guiding light in helping young adults through their addictions to sobriety with the "Dope Show," a unique interactive approach to alcohol and other drug-abuse education, as well as in his private practice in Santa Cruz, California. Alan, you left us far too soon, may your legacy carry on.

CONTENTS

When the student is ready, the teacher will appear.

- Ancient Buddhist Proverb

Introduction

My true journey started in the new millennium. Forget about Y2K, I had my own catastrophe going on, only I knew it as 'my life.'

Little did I know how much everything familiar to me would change: into a state of chaos that would eventually resolve into my world as I know it today.

You cannot comprehend the extent of my gratitude. Grateful for where I have been and what I have learned from it and grateful for everything I have today and the ability to share my wisdom.

I am a survivor. I found myself, in a single year, experiencing the death of a close relative, a divorce, a job layoff, and the death of my Mother's boyfriend of twelve years. Even my therapist said that most people would go over the edge having been through what I encountered. Yet I was still functional to the untrained eye.

At that point in my life I was self-medicated and fifty pounds heavier than today, an accident waiting to happen.

Functional, hah! Needless to say I was not a happy girl and my life reflected this. I dabbled in a few substances and some I got quite proficient in, though for some reason they never caught ahold of me. My only true demon was alcohol, the socially accepted drug of choice.

This book is a survival guide for those who may find themselves in a similar state of chaos, and who want to make a healthy change in their lives.

It is about 'my story.' What I once was, and how I went from the depths of addiction to sobriety, and onto the path of enlightenment.

I am still finding my way. The journey has been so remarkable that I would not change a thing. It is my intention to give hope to others that may be facing their own challenges. May you see yourself in some of my 'adventures' and realize that there are many wonderful options open to you if you are ready to make some changes.

Linda

Ken

He lay there. His body ravaged by the lifestyle he had learned and accepted by his alcoholic Mother. The toxins that consumed him turned his once handsome features into a man who looked to be in his 80s. He was only 57.

After losing his Mother and being abandoned by his wife, he had come to Las Vegas to die. To end the suffering of a life he never seemed to have a firm grasp on. The circumstances that brought self destruction he did not know how to free himself from.

She sat by his bedside in his room at the hospice staring down at the man lying there who provided her with a lifetime of torment. So much hatred and anger. She was now his main means of comfort. The anger and pain all seemed to melt away as he finally allowed her in, allowed her to be the one to take care of him in his final days.

These few days were decades in the making. Perhaps this was the master plan. Now at least for one the love was allowed to shine through the anger ending any karmic repercussions. A healing had occurred. The rift was over and love was the victor.

LINDA CROSE-ANDERSEN

When you possess great treasures within you, and try to tell others of them, seldom are you believed.

- Paulo Coelho - The Alchemist

A baby is born

I was born into an upper-middle class family in a small town in pre-Silicon Valley, California. The year was 1958, a time of the American dream. I was the middle of three children and lived a happy, normal childhood filled with all the wonderful trappings of the middle class. My father had his own business and brought with that, what to my mind was a very comfortable lifestyle.

My mother was a trophy wife, a younger more attractive version of dad's previous wife. There was a ten year's difference my parents' ages, which often brought on conflict. Aside from the age difference, they were normal parents for the time.

We were embarking on the turbulent 60s, the whole nation was about to change. Things were different then and so were our idols. Friday nights had us gathered around the TV to watch

Dean Martin and his Rat Pack buddies. Guys in tuxedos sexily crooning, with a cocktail in one hand and a cigarette in the other. They were smooth and always surrounded by beautiful women. Alcohol was a way of life. It certainly was in any home I visited as a kid, every home had a wet bar as standard equipment. This was our world, not wrong or right, simply the world we lived in.

Mom was the ever-present housewife. She took care of the home, she smoked, she drank, and took prescription drugs as was normal for that period in time. There was alcoholism on her side and later to find out mental illness on his. Dad never smoked and rarely took a drink.

I had an older sister and a younger brother, the only two siblings I knew of at the time. Looking back, I had a wonderful childhood. My siblings would beg to differ. Maybe it was different for them, I don't know, I always tended to blame myself for my environment, not others. I learned how to mentally escape at a very early age and as I got older I escaped via other means. My first drink was at the tender age of ten, hitting the bar at the neighbor's house and consuming shots of Crème de Menthe.

I remember family gatherings. My Mother's side of the family all lived locally and the whole brood met three specific times each year: on Christmas, Mother's Day, and my Great Grandma's birthday.

Great Grandma emigrated from Sweden at 17 and worked as a nanny until she met her husband, who was also Swedish. They had one daughter, Evelyn, who was my mother's mother. Grandma Evelyn died at an early age, leaving behind three young children who would be raised by Great Grandma. We all cherished Great Grandma. I was so blessed to have her in my life until I was close to 40. She lived alone until her 80s and died in a rest home after a stroke at age 99, just a couple months shy of her 100th birthday.

Our family gatherings were boisterous to say the least. They were generally held at my Uncle Chuck and Aunt Carolyn's house. Attendees consisted of his siblings, my mother and my Auntie Gwen and their families, their half-brothers, Jim and George and numerous young cousins.

This was a family of Scots, and the booze always flowed freely. Uncle Chuck had a bar with seats in front and even at a young age we competed to have a seat there. The Cousins were close and stayed that way until later in life when our priorities would change. This was the beginning of our 'normal,' and as we grew up and had families of our own our kids would experience the same.

I was the special child, who was meant to become the success of the brood and was sent to private school at a very young age. There I learned to speak French and read the classics, all at the ripe age of 6. I was scored with an IQ of 150 and a path of promise.

Then came the Public School system. I did not take to it well.

For some reason, most likely economic, I was soon sent to the local public school. I would love to say I flourished. Unfortunately that was far from the truth. What made things worse was that the school I initially was sent to in the 4th grade 'evicted' me and sent me to another school, further from my home. It was bad enough going to a new school, meeting new kids, and then having to go through that nonsense all over again! Kids are resilient and I proved that!

Call it boredom, lack of attention; either way the golden girl started a downward descent into mediocrity, and it was not a good place to be. Not for this girl! It seems I needed to be in the spotlight, not just another kid in the educational system. Looking back, it all makes sense now.

I wasn't popular, yet I wasn't unpopular, I just did my own thing and for some reason was always getting 'called out' or in trouble for things I did not do.

Fourth grade was my first encounter with injustice. I went into the girl's bathroom and saw a childish drawing of a naked girl and it had Rhonda written on it. Apparently I was spotted giggling at this cartoon and the next thing I know I was called into Principal's Office. I was accused of being the Artist! I didn't even know who Rhonda was, yet I was convicted of a crime I did not commit.

No fingerprints, no witnesses, no DNA, nothing! Perhaps that is why I was shipped off. Who knows? All I know is that was the beginning of a trend.

At the new school, began the period of other girls wanting to beat the crap out of me. Well, actually it was only one. Why? I don't know, maybe she smelled my nonchalant attitude and didn't like it.

Or maybe it was my way of being quick to make a clever comment or laugh. Either way, it could get me into trouble. I will never forget telling my mother about this girl who wanted to beat me up.

Mom came to pick me up at school one day and

from the description I gave her went and confronted the wrong girl! Double slam for the new kid! But you had to love Mom for her lioness' instinct. Eventually it did turn out that my tormentor and I wound up being good friends in High School. Who knew? I guess the situation changes when you are sitting at a party getting stoned together.

Looking back, junior high was pretty non-descript until the boys came into play. I was to find out all about the opposite sex in the seventh grade.

I remember going to my first dance. They called them LAYCC as they were held every other Friday at the Los Altos Youth Community Center, which happened to be situated right next to the Los Altos Police Department. My first encounter was walking in and seeing these eighth graders sitting on the floor making out and I thought "What is up with this? Gross!"

Little was I to know that my first kiss would not be with one consenting seventh grader, but with three! They all lined up and had a shot. One, I found out years later, turned out to be gay, though I won't take credit for that.

During the eighth grade I was once again to piss

off the female population when I started going steady with a guy who was in high school. The Pom Pom girls and Cheerleaders could not figure out what a high school guy would possibly see in me. It was instant resentment.

High school brought more of the same. I had a different boyfriend every week. I don't know what it was. Maybe it was the fact that 'I' was different. Far from being a girly-girl, I was just one of the boys. I guess you could call me one of the boys with 'assets.' I could certainly out-smoke and out-drink them all and be 'fun,' all at the same time. My first sexual experience was at 13 and I had definite substance abuse problems by 15. It was easy to be promiscuous when your body was being ravaged by hormones and drugs.

Believe it or not I did manage to graduate High School a semester early, at 17, though I didn't partake in the graduation ceremony. There I was, a High School graduate with no thoughts of the future and no inclination to go to college. I figured that college was where girls became secretaries and went to meet their future husbands. Not me, I had things to do, I just did not know what they were. As it was, I married at 19. So much for my thoughts of superiority!

My insights from this chapter

Everyone is born a genius, but the process of living de-geniuses them.

- Buckminster Fuller

The party years
or Babies having babies

I met my first husband, Paul, when he came out from the east coast to stay with his brother Alfie. I had dated his brother and still hung out with him and his friends in this old former Stanford frat house in Palo Alto. That visit was fate. Paul never did return to his home state of New York.

Our instant attraction was mutual and soon we were an item. I was shocked the day he got down on his knee and asked me to marry him. He was my best friend and I said yes. I was not love-struck, but in 'a lot of like.'

Right before we were to marry, he was accepted into a forestry program at a school in Grand Rapids, Minnesota. We married in May of 1977 and moved to Minnesota in August of that year so that he could begin preparing for his new career. We were caretakers of a lakeside home about 20 minutes out of town. It was a wonderful time that certainly had its challenges, both financially and logistically. I had never lived on my own before and I was having a blast; still the consummate party girl and now I had a partner in crime.

I was never the type to babysit in high school. Children just didn't interest me at that time. The topic of children was broached on occasion, though I was not up for the idea. I wanted to wait, but we soon came to the agreement that if I was to get pregnant that would be O.K. although we were not trying to conceive. The birth control of choice was condoms, due to my having issues in the past with other types of birth control.

One night in the heat of passion, we realized that our stash of condoms was depleted, yet we went ahead anyway. Six weeks later I found out I was pregnant with our first child. I think this was meant to be, since when it was time to move back to California and I was packing our things, I found one lone condom in the drawer of the nightstand. I have been a strong believer in fate ever since.

Our first Son was born in 1978. I found out I was pregnant the day before Thanksgiving. We called our families Thanksgiving Day and broke the news. My Mother always hosted the holiday so much of the extended family would be there. My Father was ecstatic; my Mother was less than thrilled. I believe her comment was, "How could you do this to me! I am too young to be a Grandmother! I expected so much more for you!" Oh well, it didn't change a thing, I was pregnant and I had this little being inside me.

I was 20 years old and scared. Scared for the future and for what I had done to my body in the past. At that time I was smoking two packs of cigarettes a day and it was not unusual for me to go through a fifth of whiskey in a night. Plus I had been diagnosed with walking pneumonia and had jumped off a moving snow mobile.

Would this baby even survive in utero? The day after I found out I was pregnant, I went clean and sober. No smoking, no drinking. I was going to be a mother and a responsible one at that! I kept that promise to myself and in July of that year I had a healthy eight-pound baby boy via C-section.

I never thought I would have another child. In my first pregnancy we had taken classes in the Bradley Method. Bradley is a breathing technique that incorporates a deeper type of breath. I wanted a birth as natural as possible. In my third trimester we were told that the baby was breach. Not only was he breach, but he was "transverse." Transverse is where the baby is butt-first, not feet-first, so needless to say this baby would come into this world via surgical means. For the longest time I felt I had failed as a woman because of this. In my mind, I could not even give birth correctly! This thought was to plague me for years.

Four years later my biological clock took over and I found myself pregnant once again. In May of 1984 I gave birth to another beautiful baby boy. This time was different. Due to circumstances I found myself having a prolonged labor, two days to be exact. Erik was born without anesthesia, without anything. Like women who work in the fields, I gave birth and walked down the hall to my room. I had found my inner strength and now knew what I was capable of.

Paul and I wound up buying a home in our old neighborhood and spent the next decade and a half making ends meet. I was 25 with a mortgage and two babies. Our boys went to the same schools in Los Altos I had attended, and even had the same pediatrician and dentist!

This was the cocaine-fueled 80s and every weekend had a party scheduled either at our house or somewhere else. They often lasted all night. Any attempt at normalcy failed. Kids sports events, playdates, were all impacted by the size of the hangover. This was our life.

Paul was happy working his Warehouse job, and his happiness was important though I longed for more. I could not expect him live my dream. We were raised differently. Him in a blue collar household, me in my white collar world. I knew that if we were going to get where I wanted to be, I needed to make it happen.

It was at that time I spoke with a Lawyer friend of mine who suggested I go back to school and get my degree. When she mentioned this to me my reaction was, "How can I do this? I won't graduate until I am 40!" She replied, "You will be 40 anyway, wouldn't you rather be 40 with a degree?" So off I went and enrolled in the local Community College. In 1999 I graduated with my AA in Social Science. I was 41.

The home we had bought had an apartment built on the side and Paul's brother Alfie came to live with us. It did not help that his brother consumed a 12 pack of beer and two packs of cigarettes daily. In the early days I had worked for Mervyns and had moved up the ladder from Christmas help to a Store Executive position. I was in my late 20's at the time and still very immature in my thinking. I had decided to have a party and invite all my Managers from the store. Though I do not remember this, I apparently told my Brother-in-Law to stay in his apartment during the party. I did not want my colleagues to meet him. I was ashamed of him. Years later after he died, the truth came out about what I had done. He had a group of friends that reasonably so thought I was quite the bitch. I was so into myself, I never really paid attention.

Alfie and I had our differences throughout the years to the point we hated each other. Yet, it was me who held him in my arms as he was taking his final breaths when the ambulance came. He died later that morning at the age of 33.

With Alfie's death came the reality of having to deal with my Husband's grief. I did not handle it well. It was hard enough for him to go into that apartment let alone pack up his deceased Brother's belongings. I forced the issue because money was tight and we had to rent the place. Truth of that matter was, we sucked at being financially mature. Yes, by the grace of God, the bills were always paid, but we managed to drink up any remaining funds.

It only got worse after Alfie died; my Husband

took on his brother's addictive behavior with a fury. I am not so sure whether Alfie's spirit entered Paul or if it was the effect of grief, but my Husband started to consume far more alcohol than he ever did prior to his Brother's death.

Many times when people go into drinking establishments there are energies that thrive on and attach to the patrons of these businesses. These are energies that had addictive issues in life and in death live vicariously through the partying habits of others. It is important to cleanse one's self after a visit to one of these places. Needless to say, our need to party increased dramatically as we left the 80s and continued on into the 90s.

The next decade was a whirlwind of affairs and decadent behavior. Much of this had to do with my own immaturity and lack of self-esteem. Why does someone who has what every girl want; a loving husband, a home, and a beautiful family have the need to seek comfort in others?

In my case, I needed that rush when you first enter a relationship, that drama that addictive personalities crave. I needed to know that I was desirable to someone else. How could I be when I was not even desirable to myself? We are so judgmental of ourselves. I look back and see pictures of this beautiful girl who thought she was unlovable because she was a little overweight. They say beauty is wasted on the young. I know this to be true because until we have the wisdom to see the true beauty in ourselves, wrinkles, rolls and all, we are incapable of radiating that beauty.

The beginning of the end was when I was caught in a passionate embrace with another. We tried to make it work for a while longer to no avail. It was on a romantic dinner cruise on the Seine in Paris when I had decided the marriage was over.

The deal was sealed when I had passed out after a ball game and Paul left a letter with my youngest Son to give to me when I woke up saying that he could not take it anymore and was leaving me. In retrospect I was proud of him for making this move. I never thought he had the guts to do it. He was the one to file the papers for the divorce as well. Apparently he had started a relationship with a woman he worked with. They are still together to this day.

I have found things always work out for the best. Had he not walked, perhaps I would be dead. I certainly would have not learned the life lessons I have spent the past decade plus learning and Paul would not have the relationship he craved, a woman who has interest in the sports events he loves so much. Arne was in College when all this came down and unfortunately Erik has suffered greatly for our actions yet lately I see a change in him. He is healing and will continue to do so if he chooses to do the work.

There were many times during my decade of being single after the divorce that I would beat myself up about being so cruel to someone who loved me so much. I often wondered if I would meet anyone who would love me as much as he did and if I did was I worthy? This was not judgment or punishment, just plain old self-realization. A feeling that was acknowledged and dismissed so that I might move on. I see my boys and I see them doing all the positive things they learned from their Dad and I am grateful for that.

Time has moved on and we have been able put the anger aside. We have come upon the time that we always looked forward to, grandchildren. We have been blessed with two beautiful granddaughters that we can get together and enjoy. The fact that we can appreciate and share in the fruits of our labor is a true blessing.

My insights from this chapter

When we are no longer able to change a situation, we are challenged to change ourselves.

- Viktor Frankl

The fall, finding self & starting over

I remember waking up with a pounding head, feeling like I had sand in my mouth. This was a daily occurrence, some days worse than others. No time to whine, as I had a job to go to. People needed me and I needed to be needed. I was functional for the most part, yet totally dysfunctional when it came to my own needs. What was this demon that consumed me? All I knew is that I needed to escape NOW! Life could no longer go on this way—wasted weekends, wasted relationships—all of it had to end.

My rock bottom came when Bob left me. He was so cold. I was in the kitchen about to start dinner and he simply came downstairs and said, "I thought I was in love with you, but I am not." He might as well have hit me over the head with a 2x4. This was a man who I gave my heart and soul to. This was the first real relationship I had since my kids had grown. I loved the fact that we could travel and had the means to do it; I loved everything we did together. I felt like an accomplished grown-up, now all that was gone and I just felt stupid.

I had started seeing Bob when he was living with someone else. Normally that was not my way to steal another woman's man. Their relationship was over although she was not ready to leave. It turns out that my meeting Bob was a blessing. His live-in moved all her stuff out and relocated to another state while we were on vacation in Cozumel. Apparently this had been in the planning for a long time.

I had been warned that lightning strikes twice or more when it comes to men who cheat, though I never thought it would happen to me. There were so many signs, even dreams.

I was 45 at the time and he expected me to learn all the sports that he loved, scuba, snow skiing; sports he had been doing for decades. I tried. I took scuba lessons while we were in Cozumel and blew my ears out. I took skiing lessons and wrenched my knee. When we had to come home early from our ski trip because I injured myself he would not even drive me to the hospital, he was too tired from the drive home. I was never allowed to bring any of my possessions to decorate the home we lived in; after all it was his mortgage.

I used to have this recurring dream about him, but the man in my dream was not Bob. Bob had a full head of hair; the man in my dream was bald.

Bob was a nice looking man. Tall, handsome—the boy next door type. He had everything I ever dreamt of at that stage of my life. He was educated with a nice house, BMW, six figure job. Everybody thought that I had struck gold! Little did they know.

I had never met anyone who drank like he did. He was a binge drinker. He liked to fill water bottles with vodka and during a binge would take his 'refreshment' to his high security clearance job. He would wake up at 4 am and start to drink. The first time my cousins ever met him he was wasted. They wanted to do an intervention! He was even too much for my party hearty family! His bottom came when, while drunk, he fell down the stairs and hurt his back. He spent a week self-medicating and I was the classic enabler who would call into work for him. Finally HR called and told him he would need a doctor's note to return to work. Still in pain, he returned with his water bottle and was caught this time. Almost 25 years on the job and this was his first offense. Amazing.

He was told by his employer that he had to go through a rehab program. There was no option.

He was 2 years away from retirement with a pension. He had a lot to lose if he chose not to comply. I kept drinking and he tolerated it. I was selfish and not ready to stop. That must have been so hard for him, especially when we traveled. As addictions go, he began to drink again and the company once again put him into rehab with a strict warning that this was the last time. He was sober when he left me. He had hooked up with another woman who had a serious drinking problem as well. He cheated on her with a sober me and in the end chose to be with her while I was visiting my son in San Diego. Even though I feel I was destined to meet Bob and be part of his life it was another man who catapulted me into sobriety. Bob was only the nudge.

At this time, I have no recollection of what his name was. He was just another guy who I had invited to my home for the possibility of something more than a one or two night stand. We were out on the patio drinking wine when he noticed how I would just zone out periodically. He finally got very angry with me and started shouting how I should get help, that I really had a drinking problem. Even then, I was willing to have sex with him, I was so far gone. He left immediately and I lost it! I could not stop the tears.

All my past experiences surfaced and brought on a torrential flow. I desperately tried to find a number for AA. I do not know if it was just me or what, but for the life of me I could not find one. I wound up being connected to some rehab facility in Florida that was ready to have someone pick me up and fly me out to their facility. I started making arrangements to go to Florida. I called my mother the next day to tell her what I had done.

My Mother had quit drinking a few years before and was always on my back about my consumption. I truly thought she would be happy about my decision. She basically told me that this was one of the most stupid things I had ever done. After she finished sharing probabilities of all the consequences and what ifs, she then told me how I should go to the hospital that she went to for help. I think that this was the beginning of a conflict between us that would last for years. We didn't know how to be a sober mother/daughter team. I was so over being told what to do, it was my time to take control over

Knowledge is a gift we take for granted. It's no different than the PJs we receive at Christmas, only to be stuffed into a drawer because we have much cooler gifts to play with. Then the day comes, you come across those stuffed in a drawer PJs and say, "Cool, I could use these!"

Stored knowledge is no different. The past decade has allowed me to discover much stored knowledge that has sat untapped for a very long time.

My Uncle Chuck used to love to share the story of how I was at the clan tent at the Scottish Games in Pleasanton and told him I wanted a shot of scotch because I was going to start rehab that Thursday. Actually, I had two shots. He always had really good scotch for the games.

Sure enough, that Thursday I entered 'The Camp,' an outpatient rehab program. That was over a decade ago and I have not had any scotch, wine or any kind of alcohol since. The thing is, I had made a decision and had chosen to work out all the garbage that made me want to drink in the first place. I believe that until you make that commitment to yourself, you will never succeed fully in sobriety. You need to confront the root cause. Sure, you may do without alcohol, but from life experience, there is nothing more uncomfortable to be around than an anger-filled dry drunk.

My most cherished friends and family who drink will never know how hard it was to be around them during social gatherings. I could have hidden and stayed away, but that would have been avoidance and that is not part of the process. You have to check-in with your feelings and ask yourself why you are having these feelings. That is how you come to terms with yourself.

You see, I know that if I was to have that glass of wine it would just lead to a bottle, then another bottle. One glass would just piss me off! Why go through all that angst? I would rather hydrate myself with water and not have to deal with the hangover than to try to limit myself to one alcoholic beverage.

It is not worth the angst or the damage to my system. I have too much respect for myself. Let the others play head games limiting (if they can) their intake and telling everyone how good they are for doing so, or not! Maybe they look at drinking as "freedom." Freedom to do what they want? There is no freedom in addiction.

I'll be candid here. Yes, sometimes I do look at someone in the table across from me savoring a glass of really good red wine and I think, *Wow! Wouldn't it be nice to be able to have that on occasion?* That is the romantic thought coming in. Then, the reality of the situation taps me on the shoulder and I realize this is a choice I have made. I am able to have that glass of wine and suffer the consequences or look at that person enjoying himself and enjoy life with them knowing that I have made the right choice for me.

I understand that not everyone has the ability to see things the way I do. It is a process, and it takes a very long time. I am not telling anyone what to do, but if any of this resonates with you, try it. All it takes is finding respect for yourself and making that choice.

When I wake up feeling good, and I look in the mirror and don't have a puffy, red face staring back at me, I know I made the right choice, for me.

I saw this late night commercial when I was in my twenties and it really had an impact on me. It was a young girl carefully putting on her make-up and the ad line was, "You can't cover up a drinking problem." Brilliant! Not that I stopped drinking at that point, but the fact that I remembered that commercial some 30 years later meant that it made an impact.

The Universe is amazing. In God's plan, our life is already predestined. Sure we can do what we can to try and change things, but life is truly in the hands of something far larger than us. All my life I worked for someone else. I was secure in a world of accomplishing given tasks and fulfilling them in a satisfactory manner. It was safe there. I could count on that bi-weekly paycheck and base my life on the amount of money I was able to bring in.

Though I was always broke and living paycheck to paycheck. I was afraid that if I left my job my life would be over. What would I do? I was barely making ends meet working for others. Many of my employers thought I rocked and would tell me they wish they had ten of me, others thought I sucked. What makes that happen to go from Teacher's Pet to insignificant?

Then it finally happened, no matter what I did it wasn't good enough. I was making mistake after mistake and forgetting important details. A less evolved individual would most likely blame it on others, however, I knew deep in my heart there was something more to it. I tried harder to be more focused but it just was not happening.

That's when I figured it out. I wasn't supposed to be there. Working for someone else served me for a time, yet the Universe had other ideas for me. Bigger and better things and it was time to get crackin'!

While I was still in the Medical Device industry, I decided to take a leap of faith and follow my dream. This dream manifested into the Wings of

Luv Center for Wellness. The center was open for a year when I realized this was not MY dream. I had allowed other practitioners I had brought in to take away my power! It got to the point where I never went into the office as I had no clients.

What was the point? I would get phone calls from one practitioner about how no one was cleaning except for him. I never had this much grief from my own children when they were growing up. My patience was frayed, I decided to take action.

Prior to my decision to 'clean house', I had contacted a dear friend of mine Maxi, to create a logo for Wings of Luv. I had been reading a book on starting your own business and decided to participate in an exercise that was in the book. The exercise was to contact friends and ask them to come up with three words when they think of you and tell you what they are.

The purpose of the exercise is to make you think. Many times we have attributes that we do not give ourselves credit for. Maxi, God love her, felt the exercise was rather silly and that when asked people would either lie to you or REALLY be candid. I replied back to her and let her in on my business and what was happening.

Being the Goddess she is, Maxi told me that I

needed help and she would provide it. The first thing she did was go to my website and erase the page where I was promoting my colleagues. No wonder I was not getting clients, I was giving away everything. I paid for ads and included these guys, promoted them on my radio show, and gave them free space at my events. I was telling the Universe I don't need anything, just give it to everyone else because apparently they need it more!

At this point I knew what I needed to do, and that was to restructure my business. My gut churned every time I thought about what I had to do. I had to regain my space but I did not want to have to break the news to the guys. Finally, I emailed them to arrange a meeting. The way things were turning out, one could not meet at all and the other could. I wanted to be done with this and tell them both at once that they had 60 days to vacate the premises, I felt that this way there would be no favoritism, not that there was.

This was making things so much harder and my stomach churned even more. I finally decided to email the one practitioner, as he requested I do so. I then called the other, and as luck would have it, he was not home. I am ashamed to say I left a voicemail. I then forwarded the email I had sent to the other practitioner and waited. I knew this was the calm before the storm.

Never again would I allow myself to be put in this position. This was a business decision. I had to make this business work; I was no longer in the mindset of working for others. I had bills to pay, a car payment, a mortgage, and a lifestyle I valued, and wanted all that I was used to, and more!

Remember how I said I was able to manifest anything I desired? Well, it happened once again in the form of two ladies who rented the space. A perfect fit! One even had her husband remodel the bathroom at no charge! I am so grateful for implementing the change.

I also found out something about myself. I had been concerned that I was a loser, as I did not have as many clients as I thought I should have. I finally came to the conclusion that my center was exactly what I had manifested! I had sent the intention of a place for alternative practitioners to practice and that is exactly what I have! *Bye, bye loser, none here!*

Now it was time for me to start a career that I had always dreamed of.

My insights from this chapter

Freedom is not the absence of commitments, but the ability to choose—and commit myself to—what is best for me."

- Paulo Coelho

A new life, a new love

I had been a single woman for 10 years; which is amazing, since I could not stand listening to my friend's advice of "Get to know yourself for at least a year before you go into another relationship." In retrospect, this was valuable advice and I highly recommend it. Sure, I had relationships, fell in love and through these experiences found myself where I am today. Married for the second time.

In my mind, we experience relationships to determine what is and is not good for us. I tell my clients who are in mourning over a relationship to take the lessons and the love and let go of the rest. Using this concept teaches us what we want in a relationship and what does not resonate, so that we can avoid this type of behavior or personality in the future.

I had been through many of these experiences in

my ten years of being single, and now decided to nix Match.com and Plenty of Fish and just let the Universe take over. I needed to go to places where I would find more spiritually-minded people. I found a Meet-Up that was no longer active, but managed to connect with the organizer. She said that she had not held one in a while as she didn't have the turnout she had expected, and had been left with the cost of the space and was not sure she wanted to do that again.

At the time, I lived in a condo complex with a cabana next to the pool that residents could reserve at no charge for private events. We agreed that this would be the venue for the next Spiritual Singles Meet-up.

We wound up having a decent turn-out of about ten people. With Meet-ups you can see ahead of time who will be attending and their contact information. I had viewed the site with no particular attraction to any one person though I remember seeing pictures of a man with a Russian name from Sao Paulo, Brazil. I thought he was OK, but no real attraction; actually my thought was "Oh, some short Russian guy who lived in Brazil."

The night of the event, when everyone gathered I did not see him. It was not until later that he showed up at the window with his motorcycle helmet under his arm and I was the one to let him in. Much to my surprise, the "short Russian guy" turned out to be a "tall, handsome, Brazilian guy" who sat across from me and stared and smiled at me all evening.

The initial plan between the event hostess and I was that all of us would meet at the cabana then go out to dinner. That plan seemed to fizzle and I passed out my business card to the group so that we could all meet in the future. I had a short chat with my future husband and found that he had four children; three in Brazil and the youngest that he had partial custody of in the U.S. He also shared that he was a grandfather and I remember commenting on what a handsome grandfather he was.

He made an excuse not to go to dinner with us, as he said he had to go pick up his 11 year old son. Apparently he thought that I was interested in someone else, which I was not. He gathered a bunch of the guys to go out and see his motorcycle and I went to my place to get the key to lock up. He approached me and I had asked if he had gotten a business card from me. He said that he thought he had and left.

When I went into the house, I was guided to write him to give him my phone number in case he was interested. Within the hour I received an email back asking me out to dinner the next evening. I replied yes. We had dinner and have been together ever since.

He took me to a local Italian restaurant. During dinner I asked what his spiritual interest was to which he replied with a big "Huh?" and I said, "You just saw the singles part" and he said "Yes." At that moment I knew the universe had stepped in. It was like we had been together forever. The comfort level was one of ultimate peace and acceptance. We had both found what we were looking for.

Our attraction to each other was not shared, especially by my family. My mother, I believe, thought that I would be single the remainder of my days—at least the remainder of hers—and relied on me to be there for her. My new situation would be bad enough had it been with someone she felt was worthy of me, let alone someone she felt was so out of my league that she could not even comprehend the attraction. And so, as they say in the famous joke, that is when the fight began.

Gregori and I met in early November of 2010. My eldest son was to be married later that month. Gregori had wanted to go with me to the wedding in San Diego, however I was still feeling him out and there was no way I was going to take him.

The family later met him that Thanksgiving and they were not impressed. Partially this was my fault as I tend to be very accepting and think that others are like me. I know now that this is so not true and it is something I constantly work on. My future husband had wanted to go and change clothes and because in my mind where he lived was so far away I talked him out of it. Big mistake! My family are very visual people and make immediate judgment on the way a person looks, especially my mother.

Gregori tried so hard to be respectful, yet all she saw was pure evil. Her daughter was being taken away and she did not like it. My brother saw an illegal alien and in his mind saw what he disliked most as he is a contractor and would see jobs that he felt should go to him going to immigrant labor.

The situation was not good. It did not help that Gregori and his son were not familiar with the American holiday.

Love is love. However, I will tell you that no matter how much you want to deny it, cultural differences always get in the way. It took me awhile to really relate to this and it was not until

I made a trip to Brazil that I really began to understand my husband. Even with that understanding our relationship could be a struggle.

When we announced our marriage is when the bomb went off! My boys were totally OK with it, as they just wanted to see their mom happy. My mother, on the other hand, was livid.

I insisted Gregori ask for my hand in marriage, as a courtesy, though once again I only made things worse; because then my Mother could expose her true feelings, which she did. I believe her exact words were "You are not marrying my daughter!"

Now you have to understand, I was 51 years old, not 16, and this was going to happen with her blessing or without it. I in no way wanted to hurt her, yet this situation was so dysfunctional. I completely understood her point of view: I was marrying a man who was an illegal alien, who ran a cleaning service. He also had four children from four different women, only the last one of which he had married. This is not what girls who are raised in Los Altos do, let alone grown women who should know better!

Gregori had visited from Brazil and had

overstayed his Visa by ten years. During that time he had created a successful cleaning service in the East Bay that on a good year would earn him $250K, although by the time I met him he had tapered down his involvement in the business by giving his ex-wife half of it. The business was no longer his focus and he was just waiting for it to die out.

Our union would lead to immigrant issues which, to be honest, never occurred to or concerned me. Eventually these were resolved, and I was to sponsor him, my stepson and a stepdaughter in Brazil who was under 18 at the time.

We were married in June of 2010. Marriage was important to the both of us. For me, I felt that I had grown up a lot in the ten years of being single and really respected the institution of marriage. And as for my husband, he felt that a girl like me was marriage material. We did not want to just 'play house' as my mother suggested.

We chose to be married in City Hall in San Francisco in the Rotunda, followed by a lunch at a nearby restaurant. We had a reception the following day in the cabana where we met. His parents had been visiting us from Brazil for the last month and we already had another Brazilian visitor living with us, so I was glad he had some support throughout the whole process.

We were scheduled to be married at one o'clock on June 4th at the San Francisco City Hall. The way it works at the City Hall is, that unless you pay big money to reserve the Rotunda for your event, it's on a first come, first served basis. So when we arrived at the venue that day and saw that there was already a previously planned event happening in the Rotunda, I was a little disappointed.

I spoke to the Angels and told them that they had found me the man I was to marry, and in doing this answered my prayers, and that wherever we were to be married would be where it was destined to happen. We had his parents, our Brazilian guest, my mother, my son and his new wife, my other son and my future husband's youngest son in tow.

What a chaotic situation! Not for the fact that my mother was doing her best to keep her chin up and that there was a language barrier between our guests and family, but because you are allowed only so many people in your party and the other bridal parties far exceeded that number. It was hot, crowded, our appointment was late, and my nerves were on edge trying to be there for everyone—and now to top it all off, I was going to be married in some tacky little room in

City Hall. Through all this I focused on staying positive.

Then it happened. We were called to the desk, and the Justice of the Peace introduced herself and asked if we wanted to be married in the room we had been assigned or in the Rotunda! I told her that the Rotunda was closed due to another event but she said that it had finished and was open for us to use. The Angels were there for me once again and the event was absolutely beautiful, even Mom was moved.

The following day we had our reception with family and friends in the cabana. The woman who was in charge of the room schedule had allowed a children's birthday party to occupy the room before our reception. Needless to say, I was not happy. It was a bad situation for both parties. For the mother who had the birthday party for her child, who had to end the party and clean-up quickly; and for us, whose help had bailed that morning leaving us to do everything ourselves. Thank God for my boys and their significant others! They were so helpful and saved the reception.

My Mother was not going to miss this day. I had invited her best friend to keep her company. My sister did not show up, as she had other plans with her partner, and my extended family had previously made plans to take a family member to Vegas for her 21st birthday. They did make sure they were represented by those spouses who did not make the trip, which was very thoughtful.

This was a very stressful time, and I took a lot of things personally with my family. I know better now and I know the boundaries. People are going to do what they feel they need to do and I am responsible for my part only.

I guess I would rather have people do what they prefer, than to give a false impression of camaraderie. This way, I too have permission to do what is my preference, though many don't get that! I guess we reap what we sow and that is the bottom line. Because I am easygoing most of the time, it seems to have given people the idea that "Linda will understand." Well, to be perfectly honest, Linda doesn't always understand. All I can do is change my reaction to the situation, which I have done in many cases—but then again, I never claimed to be perfect.

As I am writing this book, I reflect on the many challenges Gregori and I have gone through together. He was arrested by Immigration shortly after we were married. I remember being in the shower one Monday morning getting ready for work when I heard some commotion going on. I looked out my second story window and saw a guy hiding behind a tree and thought, "What the hell is going on?" I asked my stepson who was staying with us for the week and he said "I don't know, something about a visa."

My mind was so far from the concept of immigration that I thought, "I paid my Visa bill and they certainly do not come to your house when it is overdue!" I went downstairs and saw my husband sitting on the couch with a towel around him and four men in bulletproof vests and guns standing in my living room! The first words out of my mouth were "Who the fuck are you, and who is hiding behind the tree?" I was answered with "Oh, he is one of ours and have you filed with Immigration?"

The truth is, we had secured an immigration attorney, and had an appointment for that Thursday. As his parents had been visiting, we had let a month lapse before our appointment, which was within the guidelines, as I believed at that time we had three years to file. The officers handcuffed him, much to my protest, as they were concerned with Gregori's six foot two, 250 pound frame. Though there were 4 officers with guns we let them do their job. They took him to San Francisco and processed him and let him go. The fact that he has never gotten into trouble and always paid his taxes worked in his favor.

Members of my family felt he married me to get his Green Card and were corrected when they were educated on the process.

We have just passed our four-year wedding anniversary, and we have had many a bump in the road, yet many fabulous memories as well. Since we met, I have had experiences I never thought I would have and I know it is the same for him. We have issues with parenting styles, culture, money, business, many of the same things other couples struggle with. Many times I just want to throw in the towel, but then I remember the love, and that challenges are a way of life. What good is something if it is not worth finding solutions to the troubled areas.

I now have to face the issues head on instead of self-medicating and thinking that all is resolved. I have more focus and clarity, and even in those times when I feel all is lost, I have the faith to bring it all back to center. I did not have these skills a decade ago, or perhaps I did, but I certainly did not know how to access them. I am grateful for this new found ability to reach into myself and find the tools to make life work for me and my marriage. I am grateful for being given a second chance at love.

My insights from this chapter

A journey of a thousand miles begins with a single step.

- Lao Tzu

It's your party
Top 5 suggestions for sobriety

Time heals all wounds. I promise you this, as I know it to be true. When Bob left me, that was the darkest time of my life, yet also the brightest. I was in a downward spiral. People avoided me so they would not have to listen to my tale of loss, and in retrospect I don't blame them. They had seen how dysfunctional the relationship really was and were happy it had ended.

Regarding the concept of time and it's healing capabilities: a couple of years later I found a condo that I absolutely loved. I would visit this place every weekend and figuratively peed in every corner of the home to make it mine. The trouble was, it was a lot of money. But I have always been the Queen of Manifestation. Even before I knew what manifestation was I seemed to acquire things that I wanted. This home was no different.

Bob and I would take walks past the complex all

the time when we lived together. I was always curious about it and had now found a unit I intended to make my home. Yes, right around the corner from him! After moving in, one day I was on the patio which faced the street and saw a guy jogging by. I yelled out his last name and he stopped and just stared.

Now, by this time I had lost 50 pounds and gone through a make-over which eliminated my hair color of a funky red and transformed me into a blonde. Even doing move-in stuff I looked pretty hot, if I may say so. Now, not that I am into revenge however, I must admit looking good is the best form of revenge, if that is what you are into. It seals the deal that your personal power still belongs to you, and that is a huge concept.

The point I am trying to make here is that seeing him had no impact on me whatsoever. No emotions, nothing. I even invited him in to see the place and meet my boyfriend who was helping me remodel. Never in a million years when I was in the midst of my grief would I have expected an outcome such as this. So when I say, "Time heals all wounds," I mean it! As long as you are willing to let go of your 'stuff'.

I am not going to lie and say overcoming addiction is easy, because it is not. Your whole life will change, for the better. Regardless of what you think now, it will change. You will no longer be in your comfort zone. Your longtime friends will change. You will have to learn how to deal with certain social situations, including the ones that include your heavy drinking family if that is the case. Holidays and celebrations will all be different and you will have to treat them as such. You may just find them more meaningful, perhaps even discover their original intention.

 I am going to tell you right now, what works for one person does not always work for another. Take AA for example. I would always be asked to speak at meetings as I enjoy public speaking and am good at it. When I would speak, I would tell my tale of not so much woe, and I would avoid drama at any cost.

Alcoholics love drama. It feeds their inner hatred for themselves. I would talk about how I made a conscious choice to admit myself to an outpatient rehab, as I did not like the direction my life was taking. I was not there because I had abused my children, had DUIs, or had been forced by my employer to attend meetings. I was there because I thought that is what you are supposed to do when you were trying to achieve sobriety.

It would seem to me that after my talk I was always met with a "What the fuck is she doing here?" mentality, as though I did not belong because I did not bring that drama. So I ceased to go.

I went through the steps and even had a Sponsor. I did what I felt I needed to do in the program. Truth is, when I did go, I found myself going there for the cookies and coffee, and not very good cookies and coffee at that! For me, this was not a good place. I would leave a meeting wanting to go get wasted. Not all of us are a one-size-fits-all. That is what makes us unique.

AA is a fine group that has helped millions of people, but it is not for everyone. I was with Bob when he was forced into a program and saw his reaction. He is a person who does not believe in a higher power, and many don't and guess what? That's OK. Sobriety is hard enough without trying to fit a square peg into a round hole. It is a personal journey. DO NOT ever let someone force you down a path that does not fit for you. I am not kidding when I say you will become a statistic and not in a good way either.

Speaking of which, I looked into the stats for sobriety and abuse in different programs, including AA and this is what I found.

- There are approximately 88,000 deaths attributable to excessive alcohol use each year in the United States.

- This makes excessive alcohol use the 3rd leading lifestyle-related cause of death for the nation.

- Excessive alcohol use is responsible for 2.5 million years of potential life lost (YPLL) annually, or an average of about 30 years of potential life lost for each death.

Accurate reports about the success rates of 12-step programs like AA and NA are notoriously difficult to obtain. The few studies that have attempted to measure the effectiveness of the program have often been contradictory. Fiercely protective of their anonymity, AA forbids researchers from conducting clinical studies of its millions of members. But the organization does conduct its own random surveys every three years. The result of AA's most recent study in 2007 were promising.

According to AA, 33 percent of the 8,000 North American members it surveyed had remained sober for over 10 years. Twelve percent were sober for 5 to 10 years; 24 percent were sober 1 to 5 years; and 31 percent were sober for less than a year. Alcoholics Anonymous, the organization that all 12-step programs are modeled after, does keep a record of their success rates, but in terms of the different lengths of sobriety time amongst its active members, there are no statistics that show success versus failure. In 2007, the average length of sobriety was eight years. By all accounts, this is indicative of long-term success. Other statistics include:

- Sober less than a year: 31 percent
- Sober for one to five years: 24 percent
- Sober for five to ten years: 12 percent
- Sober for more than ten years: 33 percent

Now you may ask, "Who the hell is she to dis a fine institution such as AA?" To which I would reply, "I am not trying to dis AA." I am just trying to prove a point: to each his own, do what feels right for you and don't feel guilty about it. Like I said, "It's your party."

The next five chapters are written as suggestions for creating and maintaining your sobriety. They are as follows:

- ➢ Don't Keep Re-Creating Your Story
- ➢ Never Give Up
- ➢ Live in the Now
- ➢ Find and Make a Connection
- ➢ Acknowledgement is Everything

These concepts have been, and still are, very helpful in getting me through the process and are what keeps me sober to this day. It is my intention and my hope that you find something in the following chapters that resonates with you, that you may use on your journey in sobriety, or simply in search of a better life.

My insights from this chapter

Am I doing this from fear or love? When we are in fear, there is no room for love, and when we are in love, there is no room for fear.

- A Course in Miracles

Don't keep recreating your story

I was tired of being fat and stupid. A major relationship in my life had just ended and I was headed on a downward spiral. I knew a change had to be made, something had to be done about my life. My drinking had never sent me in the direction of being abusive to my children or racking up DUIs or even worse killing anyone. The only recipient of the pain and suffering was me and it had to stop.

My kids thought our life was normal, that everyone consumed a couple bottles of wine in the evening and after a night's sleep went to work and carried on what seemed to be a functional, productive life. The issue is, it was not; not functional and not productive—and it took years to get that way.

With that said, this was my story. Valid? Then, yes. Now, no. I lived for years blaming myself for choosing alone time to drink instead of going to my boy's school functions and games.

I always had a good excuse. Then, when my eldest son became captain of his high school football team and I did not have a clue due to my lack of presence, I discovered a great hammer to beat myself over the head with! It wasn't until I had gone through the steps, and was apologizing to my boys about what an awful Mother I had been, that it was brought to my attention, that it just did not matter!

My youngest bluntly told me, "Mom stop beating yourself up!" The truth was, like me, this is what they knew, this was their life and they accepted life as such. Just like me! These were happy boys. It was then I accepted the fact that I am no longer that person. Even when I was that person I was just doing the best I could at the time. I still have incidents that creep into my memory on occasion but I merely dispel them by saying, "Yes, that sucked, but I am no longer that person. What I did was my best at the time, I know better now."

Drunks love drama, that is their connection to life. What they do not realize is that once that connection is severed, is when life truly begins— once we get to the root cause of why we need to self-medicate! When we find that root cause, the issue no longer exists.

Let your 'stuff' go! I can't stress this enough. When we keep those thoughts and feelings inside, it harms no one but ourselves. One of my favorite quotes from Buddha is, "It is like drinking poison and waiting for the other person to die." Make sense? Guilt is the lowest vibration we can have, raise your vibration and let your 'stuff' go.

Yes, I know; it's easy to say. Does it make more sense if you know that, to this day, I still struggle with the issue of letting go? The other day during my meditation, an event came to mind that happened 25 years previous. I shed some tears and asked the Angels to take it away and they did.

WE ALL DO OUR BEST AT THE TIME! I cannot stress that enough. Once we take ownership of these feelings, we as the owner have the right to dismiss them. Forgiveness is key. If you cannot find it in your heart to forgive the offending party, then try forgiving yourself for the way you reacted to the act. Many times we forget that we too are a part of the equation. Not victims, just a participant. We all have a lot more power than we think!

So when I say, "Don't keep re-creating your story," what I mean is, every time you think of the event, the issue, whatever, it re-creates the moment. Who needs that? Release and move on. Life brings enough, we will always have stuff to work through. Think of it as a de-clutter technique, like on your work area. Once you have sorted through all the paperwork that has resided there for ages and tossed what you no longer need, you have the ability to breathe, have focus.

Over time, the process will need to be done again, except that this time it will be easier, with less stuff, and it will continue to get easier and easier provided you take the time to do the work.

My insights from this chapter

He has not learned the lesson of life who does not every day surmount a fear.

- Ralph Waldo Emerson

Never give up

Every year I help out the local Fire Brigade by soliciting raffle items from local merchants for the Annual Cioppino fundraiser. This year I was feeling a little out of sorts at having to bare my soul and ask for donations but I knew it was a good cause and ventured on. I had already visited a few businesses and left information for them to contact me about a donation. This particular day the first business I went to turned me down. I told myself I was NOT going to take this personally and ventured on.

I stopped by the local Ace Hardware to pick up some personal items which I had trouble locating in the store. I finally looked at one of the sales guys and said, "I give up! Can you tell me where I might find....?" He immediately told me to "Never give up" and walked me over to the aisle where I found what I was looking for. I had taken the previous encounter personally!

As I stood in line to pay I thought perhaps I should ask the store manager if they might have an item to donate. I had never solicited this particular business and thought "I will go out of my comfort zone on this one. After all the man had said, "Never give up!"

I was led upstairs, where a sweet gal who had a severe handicap was more than eager to help. She said these requests normally take about 4 weeks but that she would see what she could do. It turned out they had a chainsaw they were willing to donate and she would arrange to get it to me in a couple days. I was stoked! What a fabulous raffle item! I then went to my car and turned on the radio and out came the song, "It's Always Darkest Before the Dawn" by Florence and the Machine. How appropriate!

After hitting the downtown for a couple more donations that were awesome as well, I proceeded down Highway 1 towards home. The traffic seemed congested and it looked like there might be an accident on the highway. I spotted a lit-up Highway Patrol vehicle following a large truck with words on the side of it stating that the truck was escorting a disabled Vet on his cross-country journey. As I began to pass the truck I saw a man with prosthetics on both legs riding a bicycle alongside his escort and another Highway Patrol vehicle leading the way.

I'll tell you, after this morning, did my thinking and priorities change! Nothing like a blatant cosmic slap to show you what a whiner you are. There are challenges around every corner, but they are a whole lot easier to deal with when you are present and in a place of gratefulness, and sobriety brings presence and gratitude.

I was flying home from a Caribbean cruise. My husband and I were heading for our seats which were in the very last row of the plane when I noticed a man sitting there already. I said, "Excuse me but I believe those are our seats." The man said, "Yes they are, but I like this side of the plane better." I looked over and the last row on the other side was completely empty so I said, "OK, we will sit here but if anyone claims these seats you will need to move."

He agreed and we left it at that. For some reason his attitude really pissed me off. Maybe it was the fact that I felt he 'took' something of mine or that he got his way and I did not. After we secured ourselves in our seats a man came by and asked our neighbor if he could take the window seat if no one else was seated there. The man told him, "No, I want to stretch out and sleep." Once the plane was in the air I turned and asked the man, "Do you always get what you want?" to which he replied "Yes, I do."

At that very moment I felt a huge shift. What a concept: to be clear and upfront about your needs and desires! I always thought I had that concept nailed, but this guy brought it to a whole new level of clarity. His actions could be perceived as being selfish, yet I saw the opposite. Everyone had their needs met, he was not taking anything from anyone. Yes, courtesy leads us to believe that it is of social value to give up our comfort for the comfort of another, perhaps not.

Most of us are so afraid we are going to hurt feelings or seem selfish that we put our own needs to the wayside. I am famous for this. This encounter really opened my eyes in that with a simple statement of truth, with no hostility, and no agenda, he could get his point across. This is a key concept for all of us, especially when sobriety is new. The bottom line is, you will have good days and you will have not so good days, go for what you want and never give up!

My insights from this chapter

Because I don't live in either my past or my future. I am interested only in the present. If you can concentrate always on the present, you'll be a happy man.

-Paulo Coelho, The Alchemist

Live in the now

I went to an event one afternoon where Doreen Virtue, PhD, was the speaker. A woman in the audience stood up to speak and was attempting to jog Doreen's memory about meeting her at another event. Doreen simply told her, "Darling, I'm sorry, I live in the now." I loved that! The woman I was with at the event thought that it was the rudest remark ever. Why? I asked myself if it would have been better for her to say, "I have spoken to and with thousands of people since that event, and no, I do not remember you!"

This brings us to suggestion #3, "Live in the Now."

When I am feeling a lack, scared, worried, or having a full blown pity party, a bit of clarity peaks through that causes me to come to the conclusion that I am really in a pretty good place!

If I take the time to look at where I am at one particular moment in time I always feel a sense of gratitude. If I am concerned about the bills I can't pay, I sit and say to myself, "OK self, at this very second you have a roof over your head, people who love you, a healthy body, and well-adjusted kids, there is no lack, nothing to worry about!" You see, I know I am taken care of now, and for always. Sometimes I just need a reminder. Even though the bill is still due, my perception towards it has gone from lack to acceptance and guess what? It always gets paid.

Living in the now is especially important for those of us with substance abuse issues. The biggest deterrent to sobriety, in my mind, is the thought that you will never have another drink, which is a dose of reality that many do not want to face. Reality is, if you want to stay sober you won't drink. If you are "In the now", you don't want to drink because you know that the one drink will lead to another, and if you truly value your sobriety you know that this is not an option.

I used to always have something on the back burner. I had an intense need to have something to look forward to. Why? Perhaps that made me feel complete or that there was something good coming in the future, but then the day would come and the event was gone and I would be busy planning something else, I never allowed myself to "Live in the now" and enjoy the moment. My life got much more 'alive' once I started to embrace the moment. There are many moments in a day and a lot of happiness can be experienced in that time.

This is not an easy exercise, this is decades of behavior modification. I encourage you to quit waiting for the future to be happy. Quit waiting for "I will be a lot happier when I just…" Personally, I would much rather have my reward now, today, than wait for something that may never come. You won't have to wait, you can have it now and embrace the feeling of true enjoyment!

My insights from this chapter

All man's troubles derive from not being able to sit quietly in a room alone.

- Blaise Pascal

Find and make a connection

I have always had a Guardian Angel. How do I know? It was just something matter-of-factly mentioned by my Mother. In fact she would say it often though one morning I was given the reason to validate my Mother's words.

I believe I was about seven when I awoke out of a sound sleep and went to my bedroom window. We lived on a cul-de-sac, and my window faced the middle of the street. Little did I know that what I saw would change me forever.

There was a beautiful woman with long blonde hair floating down the middle of the street. Her hair and long white gown billowed in the breeze. Except that it was a balmy summer evening with no breeze at all that I could see. Yet my vision encapsulated a flowing being all the same. I stood there mesmerized and just as quickly as she arrived, she disappeared.

The next morning I could not wait to tell my

Mother of my experience. When I finished my story, she very simply said, "Linda, that was your Guardian Angel." This is the way it was between her and me. Other parents would have put an end to such thoughts by throwing some reality in.

I was so fortunate to be raised in a household of acceptance. You see my great grandma was a medium and a member of the Spiritualist church in San Francisco. I spent much of my youth with weekly visits to Grandma's house, eating homemade cookies, drinking coffee loaded with cream and sugar, and hearing about who had been brought from the other side at the weekly séance. This kind of talk would give most kids nightmares, but not us. It was what we knew, our world and we were told not to share it with others.

Years later, I discovered the Angelic realm by accident. When I first "came out of the closet" with my spiritual gifts I took up the Tarot. Tarot is a wonderful divination tool, however it tends to scare people who do not know it's true meanings and origins. One day I was at my mentor's house giving her a reading and she brought out these Angel cards by a woman named Doreen Virtue, PhD. I will tell you with all honesty that I thought these to be the dorkiest things ever, yet they caught my attention.

Afterwards I was guided to do some research on Dr. Virtue and I saw that she was giving one of her Angel Intuitive trainings in her home base of Kona, Hawaii. I seriously considered making the trip, however I had just began a new job and thought it to be a little irresponsible to run off to Hawaii for week to chat with the Angels. In my research, I did find that Doreen's Son Charles was giving a slightly different course in Sedona, Arizona over the weekend. This was doable, so I signed up.

I don't mind telling you that this weekend changed my life. Things have always come easily to me, yet now I have this inner peace that all will be taken care of now and for always. Sure, I have my out of control stressful times, but like Louise Hay says, "Stress is a fearful reaction to a situation." We all have fearful times and it is comforting to know that I can reach out to my loving posse.

So now you know, Angels are my connection. I realize that not everyone reading this book finds the Angelic realm to be believable. Once again, that's OK! It is really important that you find some kind of higher source, a connection. This could be anything. It could be your living room chair! If that spot brings you to a place of true peace and being, by all means go for it! You have to go with your intuition on this one. Have an open mind and know there are choices, don't just do what others tell you to do. You really need to FEEL that whatever you choose is the right connection for you.

I am a Metaphysical Minister, I do not believe in organized religion. I have never read the bible with the exception of a children's version when I was young. Yes, I believe in God, I just do not believe in using a source to control others. 'Nuff said. I have found everything I need in the study of metaphysics. The Merriam-Webster's Concise Encyclopedia defines metaphysics as follows.

A branch of philosophy that studies the ultimate structure and constitution of reality—i.e., of that which is real, insofar as it is real. The term, which means literally 'what comes after physics,' was used to refer to the treatise by Aristotle on what he himself called 'first philosophy.' In the history of Western philosophy, metaphysics has been understood in various ways: as an inquiry into what basic categories of things there are (e.g., the mental and the physical); as the study of reality, as opposed to appearance; as the study of the world as a whole; and as a theory of first principles.

A connected belief system is what keeps us sober. I know this to be true. I also know that certain forced belief systems are what keep many people who wish to achieve sobriety out of groups that might otherwise be of value to them. Like I said before, find what resonates and FEELS good to you and you will be just where you need to be.

My insights from this chapter

If you are distressed by anything external, the pain is not due to the thing itself but your own estimate of it; and this you have the power to revoke at any time.

- Marcus Aurelius

Acknowledgement is everything

Sometimes I get sad for no reason. I guess we all do. I had weaned myself off of all meds that I had been on, one being Effexor for depression. This is a nasty, nasty drug when not taken properly or stopped suddenly. I had started antidepressants decades prior to mask the effects of what alcohol was doing to my body. The anxiety and dizziness was all due to the havoc being caused to my nervous system and blood pressure from the alcohol. Now you are told NOT to drink when taking these meds. But hey, I was a professional abuser. The rules did not apply to me!

When we had sold my condo and bought the new house in the Redwoods, it turned out we would have a month living out of a suitcase in a Motel 6. This was not my ideal situation, though with little money and few other options it was the way our life would be for the next few weeks. To kill time we decided to travel a bit.

The day we were to be out of the condo, I had to work and had asked my husband to supervise the few remaining items in the house to go into storage. I had left our packed bags in the upstairs bedroom, not giving them another thought, since to me—packed bags—we were traveling—obvious.

That night he picked me up to take me to a hotel near the airport since we were taking an early flight to Miami for the weekend. I had meticulously packed suitcases for myself, him, and my stepson for the trip. When he came to pick me up, I asked where my suitcase was. He looked at me blankly and said, 'What suitcase? Everything went into storage."

"Fabulous!" I said. "All my clothes, personal items, and my meds are in that bag!"

I frantically tried calling the storage place, with no luck. They were not going to open the gate until their normal business hours. Too bad if everything we owned was in that storage unit. Too bad that our flight was leaving San Francisco the same time that they were opening in Palo Alto. Needless to say, the situation sucked!

Once I settled down, I was able to look at this as

an adventure. We would go to Miami, buy a few clothes and toiletries, and it was only for the weekend, I could do without my meds. Not! I had never been so sick in my life! I went to CVS in Miami. I had gotten scripts at that chain locally before and thought I would not have an issue. Apparently the script had expired and the Pharmacist treated me like some kind of junkie.

I was really sick by now. We had scheduled a trip to Cape Canaveral but I ended up staying behind. I tried hot baths, massage, a walk on the beach. Nothing made me feel better. What was this toxic substance I had been poisoning my body with? Surely, it was not the cure-all for depression, as at times I was still very depressed.

After I got home and stabilized, I made the decision that a major cleanse was in order. Slowly, I broke my pills into small pieces. After a period of several months I weaned myself off of them. Now, I do not recommend you do this on your own. I have been in the Pharmaceutical Industry for decades and am very aware of how these drugs metabolize in the system. Doing this without a doctor's care or the proper knowledge could be fatal and is not recommended. Did I mention that I am a professional? I did it anyway.

The act was worthwhile for me. It has caused me

to have to deal with my 'stuff' both mentally and physically. Understand that by this time I had been sober for a decade. This caused me to have to constantly check-in with myself. It is work, important work and like all of us I am a constant work in progress. Knowing this brings a certain clarity that lessens the anxiety when I get overwhelmed.

Too many times we go through life with issues from our past that dilute our happiness. I got over the fact that daddy didn't buy me a pony years ago, yet still the stuff seems to always surface and I deal with it appropriately.

Acknowledgement is a beautiful thing. It's when we stuff down and hold on to things that emotions and feelings become toxic. I often have clients that come to me with issues regarding their parents. The problem is, that these clients are well over 50 and we are addressing issues that happened to them before age 11. That's 40 or so years of holding something in! That's a lot of negative energy being stored internally. No wonder life isn't working for them! They are a vessel of toxicity.

In many cases the 'offender' is no longer alive, and even if they are, there is really no need for confrontation. Sometimes adults, parents, friends, whatever, say things that they don't mean to hurtful or offensive. In many cases if you have the opportunity and take the time to discuss the issue with the person they will be shocked that their comment had such an effect! The important part is that you forgive that person and forgive yourself for the way you handled the situation. It still may take some work, but just try it and feel how cleansing it can be. Then be sure to forgive yourself for holding on to it for so long and making yourself feel bad.

Things happen for a reason, even sad things. We need to look at the situation and ask, "What is the lesson in this?" Blame gets us nowhere, clarity brings us peace.

My insights from this chapter

From the standpoint of daily life, however, there is one thing we do know: that we are here for the sake of each other— above all for those upon whose smile and well-being our own happiness depends, and also for the countless unknown souls with whose fate we are connected by a bond of sympathy. Many times a day I realize how much my own outer and inner life is built upon the labors of my fellow men, both living and dead, and how earnestly I must exert myself in order to give in return as much as I have received.

- Albert Einstein

Don't just listen to me
Words of wisdom from angels among us

I subscribe to an email blast "Notes from the Universe" by Mike Dooley. I just love getting these messages. Even though I know they are meant for thousands. I found them to be so appropriate, especially when facing sobriety.

Linda, it's simply a matter of applying who you already are to what you now face. That's all that matters. Because by design, who you are is always the greater.

Proudly yours,
The Universe

Then he always throws these gems in at the bottom of the page mixed in with the advertisements. Like this one.

Linda, you will one day laugh at all that now scares you. Like a spotted hyena.

So, as I was writing this book, I thought, *Rather than just reading my insights, it would be value added to have other people share their insights.* So I asked a number of people the question, "What was the defining moment when you made the decision to venture into sobriety, and what tools do you use to keep yourself sober?" Here are a few of the stories I received.

Juliana
Sao Paulo, Brazil

I can't say the exact time when I quit smoking pot, but I know it was not a strong decision. I had made best friends smoking, and I didn't want to break these relationships. I had to admit, smoking wasn't the same, the effect wasn't the same, the need wasn't the same. I had only the habit, and a vague memory of the good times associated with it. I decided to fool myself, I decided not to tell myself that I was quitting smoking, yet I didn't go out to smoke, didn't call friends to smoke, didn't buy it, didn't have it. I removed the space and the time that smoking had taken up in my life.

One time I was caught by the authorities with pot, it was a traumatic experience, and I collaborated with it, because I was unprepared and sensitive. Then the weight of illegality hit me as it never had, then smoking wasn't the same. It took 6 months until I accepted that continuing to smoke was making it harder for me to overcome the fear that my contact with the law had created.

After I quit, I realized that even when I'm not high it leaves remnants in me that continue to disconnect myself from reality. After some time without pot, I realized how important it is to be in the present. Not only what is in your head, but that you have a physical body pegged to reality, it doesn't matter what, you can't get rid of it.

Wes
San Jose, CA

I didn't have a drinking problem. I had never received a DUI. I had never had an alcohol-related accident and had never called in sick to work. I enjoyed drinking and often stated that I worked hard and played hard. Weekends were toasted upon getting off work and continued until late Sunday night. This was known publicly. What was not known was that there were empty brandy bottles stashed in my golf bag and secretive drinking of a daily bottle of champagne. No problems here. Until a series of events culminated in a perfect storm of consumption.

It was a Tuesday evening. The painful consequences of oral surgery, prescription Vicodin, a dinner fight with my soon to be fiancée and a bachelor's apartment with nothing but a half gallon bottle of vodka and some infuriatingly bad election returns on TV all conspired to trigger the excessive intake of more Vicodin washed down with copious amounts of vodka. After a few hours, I realized I was far over the edge. I was ignored by a call for help to my girlfriend and placed a barely coherent call to 911 at about 10:30.

I was awakened by the removal of something obstructing my throat and mouth. I was in a hospital, and, espying a clock on the wall, noted that it was 4:30. I assumed it was Wednesday in the AM. It was actually Friday afternoon— almost three lost days in an induced coma. 911 had responded to a call that I really don't remember. My blood alcohol level was .44, my stomach was pumped and I was taken to ICU. Somehow, my girlfriend was with me when I was revived and related as best she could what had transpired. The gravity of the situation was not lost on me: I had been close to death when the paramedics arrived.

When a psychiatrist stopped by to speak with me, he bluntly asked if I would consider going to Rehab. I broke down in tears and said emphatically, "Yes." He followed this by asking if I would consider attending 'Betty Ford', even though it was very expensive. With no hesitation, I said that I did not care how much it cost, I needed help and would do whatever was required, irrespective of price tag.

I remained in ICU for three days and, as it turned out, was not able to be admitted to the Palm Springs clinic, but could be admitted to a nearby, secluded, 30-day program.

That was my moment of clarity and the defining moment of my ensuing sobriety. I was attentive in all aspects of the Rehab and received un-expected, but profoundly beneficial support from my girlfriend and her family. I was initially advised that I would have to get new friends, change jobs and transition from Rehab to a Sober Living Environment and it all made sense to me. But as I continued with the daily discussions, the writing assignments, the group activities and the AA Meetings, I realized that I was not only understanding the lessons but internalizing them. I began to realize that my problems were not my friends or job, but solely my choices. I could return to my life, with conscious and diligently applied behavioral changes.

And I am sober today. I have been able to maintain this for 2794 days- nearly 7 1/2 years. I keep track of the days because it keeps me focused. I carry my Recover Medallion with the Roman Numeral VII and every morning, remind myself that I was sober the previous day, with the goal of remaining so today. I am painfully aware of how close I came to dying, but marvel in my daily clarity and have come to love Mondays, because for countless years, they were gilded with hangovers and 'brown bottle flu.'

I have since lost jobs, been divorced, lost both parents and dealt with all manner of adversity, and can honestly say that not once have I been tempted or even considered having a drink. I attend parties, even open wine and pour drinks, without a trace of desire. I do take this one day at a time, but if I knew one sure thing; I would say that my continued sobriety is a given.

Angel
Martinez, CA

My story begins like millions of other addicts. I come from a long line of physical, emotional and substance abuse, so it was no surprise that I became addicted to drugs and alcohol early in my teens. For me it was a way to hide from the pain. Don't get me wrong, I had very loving parents, but considering how they were raised, they did the best they could. I learned later in life that to point fingers and wear the victim role serves no purpose in my own personal evolution.

As a teenager, drinking and doing drugs was for the most part accepted. Everyone I knew did it and it was my way of being part of the tough or rebellious crowd. It seemed as long as I got good grades and didn't get in trouble with the authorities, it was okay. Well not okay, but at least I wasn't running with a gang and robbing people. As long as I was only hurting myself, my parents could deal with it.

I guess being the baby of the family, I got away with a lot more. So I learned: color inside the lines, have good manners and don't be an idiot, and I could get as wasted as I wanted. This served me well as I grew into an adult.

I graduated high school (had a beer kegger party for my graduation party!), went on to junior college and worked at the same time. I was seen as a good girl, a reliable employee, so easy to get along with, no one knew my secret. Eventually I fell in love with and married someone like me. We called ourselves 'functioning alcoholics'. We worked hard, paid our bills and built the perfect life as the perfect couple. No one knew our secrets and there were no problems, at least that's how it appeared to the outside world.

In 1997 everything changed for me. My perfect world started falling apart. I started getting psychic readings from a shaman friend of my sisters. That led to my first spiritual healing experience.

I got what in Native American medicine is called a 'soul retrieval.' I honestly believe that's where my life truly began. During this type of healing, parts of your soul that are lost due to trauma are brought back and any dark or negative energy is released. Shortly after that, I had an emotional breakdown including a full day of crying uncontrollably, panic attacks and I was even agoraphobic (the fear of outside) for a while, which was a real trick dealing with that and working full time. I thought I was losing my mind. As I look back, what I was losing was the darkness that had consumed my life. I went into counseling and began meds to control my panic attacks and depression. I reached desperately to be 'normal' like everyone else, but the truth was that 'normal' was a lie and it was quickly on its way out.

In September of 1999, my husband of 14 years and I separated and we sold our house. On tax day of 2000, I was officially divorced. I was on my own for the first time in my life and ready to begin again.

The drinking and partying continued with a new group of friends. I juggled my newfound spirituality while still feeding the addict. The recreational drugs had faded away mostly but the drinking reached a whole new level. This is how it went for the next few years, to those on the outside I had everything. On the inside, I was a lonely, sad person looking for a better way.

In 2005 my soul's calling showed itself. I was compelled to go to a holistic fair in a town about 20 miles away. The last fair I went to, I had a reader tell me that I was a healer and that I had a gift for healing others. She said she wouldn't advise massage therapy for me, but said I should look into Reiki (energy healing). This really touched me on a deeper level inside and rang true, so the next step was to find a teacher. Off to the fair I went in search of my new teacher. Now, anyone who has experienced panic attacks or agoraphobia knows going for a drive a distance away is no easy task, but I couldn't shake the feeling that this was important. At the fair, I didn't meet my teacher personally but was drawn to a brochure.

After looking at the prices, I thought, I can't afford this, put the brochure down and walked away. Or I should say, I tried. As I walked out the front door of the hotel where the fair was being held, a voice in my head stopped me. It said, Are you crazy?! Go back and get that brochure!

No matter how I tried to resist, it was no use. I went back inside and grabbed the brochure. I called the next day and began the journey to not only learning how to heal others but healing myself.

The years that followed were filled with intensive healing work on myself. I spent many hours on my healer's table fighting the darkness that lived in me. I witnessed many demons, some seen by me, others unseen. I discovered the love that God, the Universe, the Angelic Realm and all spiritual beings have for us through the healing touch of my healer. There were many hurdles; many times I lived in what is called 'the dark night of the soul,' which was a time of self-reflection and exploration. I also experienced so much love and joy that I never thought possible.

What seemed impossible was suddenly possible as I healed old wounds and forgave myself and others. I found that the more I opened to that higher love of spirit the more love I received from them.

During this time, I learned Reiki I. By the time I learned Reiki II, my life took an even more dramatic turn in finding the joy in healing others. When I learned Reiki III, I no longer felt the need or desire to drink alcohol or even the need to hide from any pain that came into my life.

The old me had been replaced with a person that lives in service to others and finds joy and miracles in everyday life. Today, my greatest joy is helping others in the journey to themselves. There are still challenges in my life, in all our lives, but now I look at them through different eyes. I don't regret the past, I embrace it. Now I show others who are searching that love is possible even when all seems lost. True peace comes from when we love and accept all we are.

My insights from this chapter

If one advances confidently in the direction of his dreams, and endeavors to live the life which he has imagined, he will meet with a success unexpected in common hours.

- Henry David Thoreau

Further down the road

- I used to think that all conversations revolved around me.

- I used to get a feeling in my gut like the world was over whenever I made a mistake.

- I used to not be present.

- I used to drink to cover my true gifts and self.

- I used to drink to hide behind the facade of being one of the gang.

- I used to have this intense feeling of need while driving home from work craving that first sip of wine.

- I used to give far too much to people that did not appreciate me or my actions.

- ➢ Now I don't need the attention from others because I know I am a perfect child of the Universe.

- ➢ Now I take the lessons from my mistakes and learn from them and know that it is the other guy's issue.

- ➢ Now I live a life of complete presence one moment at a time.

- ➢ Now I cherish my gifts and think I am pretty awesome.

- ➢ Now I feel compassion for those who abuse themselves for the acceptance of others.

- ➢ Now I give only to whom I choose.

I have learned that I am responsible for my own happiness. People rely on others far too much. Thoughts such as, *I know he truly loves me through the gifts he buys me.*

No, no no! That is so not it!

My mother would always talk about the Marquis diamond ring she dreamt about and how my father never bought her one. Dad bought some pretty beautiful pieces for her which she always returned.

I asked her one day if it would have really made a difference if he had bought her that ring. Would that mean that he loved her more? I was a little taken back when she adamantly said "Yes, if he truly loved me he would have bought that ring because he knew how much I wanted it."

Did he really? Did he really know that it would have made that much of a difference in their relationship, in her being? I don't think so. The bottom line is that if a piece of jewelry was that important to her, she should have gone out and bought it herself. Had she done this she would have skipped a whole lot of resentment and had a big piece of bling to flash.

You see, you don't need someone else to make you happy! Gifts are great on occasion, but not when expected. My husband and I never celebrate Valentine's Day. After so many years of having the mindset that I was not truly loved or appreciated because I did not get an overpriced bouquet and a reservation at a packed dinner house for the V-day, I finally came to the conclusion it just did not matter. It took a decade of being single to finally figure this out. If I want flowers I will go out and buy them, if I want bling, I'll go out and buy it and guess what? I will get exactly what fulfills ME! A beautiful gift to self.

In my husband's culture they rarely give cut flowers, instead, we will drive down the road and he will say, "Look at that beautiful field of flowers, I grew them for you!" Cheesy, yes, but it makes me smile every time! I know he really wants to show his love when he suggests we dine out, because it is not very often, or when he schleps hay down the hill for my animals, or fixes something around the house. Then I know he is truly doing something just for me.

I am now free to love. I am free to make choices. The road has been long and will continue, yet now I look forward to the journey. The destination will come in time. Until then, I walk this path with love in my heart and a smile on my face. Nothing would make me happier than to know that someone might read these words and find value in them. Know that these words gave them hope and faith to find light in their time of darkness and to emerge as a phoenix into a world of light!

Embrace yourself, embrace all you are and how you have given yourself the gift of unconditional love by choosing to value your body and live a life of sobriety.

My insights from this chapter

Your time is limited, so don't waste it living someone else's life. Don't be trapped by dogma - which is living with the results of other people's thinking. Don't let the noise of other's opinions drown out your inner voice. And most important, have the courage to follow your heart and your intuition.

- Steve Jobs

About the author

As a natural intuitive, Linda began her intense mission to learn all things metaphysical, discovering her true passion of bringing wellness awareness to each individual, and empowering them with the wisdom of their own wellness through body, mind, and spirit.

She is the former founder of the Crose Center for Wellness and Personal Empowerment and also helps people achieve their dreams through facilitating their purchase or sale of homes on the Coast and in the San Francisco Bay Area.

Linda is a native Californian and product of the Silicon Valley, who currently resides in La Honda, California with her husband and stepson, her dogs and alpacas.

A Special Thanks to …

Diane Gysin, author of *Healing Bodies Healing Souls*
Healing Bodies Healing Souls Wellness Center, Fremont, CA
HealingBodiesHealingSouls.com

Belinda Farrell, author of *Find Your Friggin' Joy*
Huna Practitioner, Reconnective Healing Practitioner
HunaHealing.com

William K. Wesley, JD, MBA, Top Performance Coach,
author of Full Life Balance: *The Five Keys to the Kingdom*
FullLifeBalance.com

44591241R00081

Made in the USA
Charleston, SC
29 July 2015